D1706237

Then...
SEEDS OF SPIRITUAL LINEAGE

Then...

SEEDS OF
SPIRITUAL
LINEAGE

BY
ROB HOSKINS

Then...
Seeds of Spiritual Lineage
Published By Book of Hope International

© 2001 by Rob Hoskins
International Standard Book Number 1-890525-70-7

Cover design by J. David Ford and Associates

Scripture Quotations are from:
The Contemporary English Version (CEV)
copyright © American Bible Society 1991, 1992, 1995
unless otherwise noted

Also quoted: The New International Version (NIV)
copyright ©1973, 1978, 1984 by International Bible Society

ALL RIGHTS RESERVED
No part of this publication may be reproduced, stored in a
retrieval system, or transmitted, in any form or by any means
— electronic, mechanical, photocopying, recording, or
otherwise — without prior written permission

Printed in Mexico.

For Information:
Book of Hope
3111 SW 10th ST
Pompano Beach, FL 33069
www.bookofhope.net
www.spirituallineage.com

Table of Contents

To Kim,
who is part of my heritage,
always my oasis,
and maker of my home —
great is your reward.

Acknowledgments

I wish to thank Bruce Wilkinson for helping awaken the nation to the promises in God's Word

I especially want to thank my writing partner Jaxn Hill for her wonderful gifting as a wordsmith and story-teller.

Thanks to every Book of Hope partner who bears fruit, much fruit and fruit that will last.

Preface

I asked, and it didn't happen. I'd been asking for a year and a half as my father-in-law laid in a coma. This immaculately elegant, proud man whom I loved for his virtue, passion and honesty, died.

I asked, and it did happen. I'd been asking for two years as my father battled colon cancer. When my hope was gone, suddenly, on a January Sunday morning, it happened, and healing was his.

Jesus makes some outrageous claims, none more fantastic or difficult to believe than His last instructions to His disciples before His death and resurrection found in John 14-16.

"Ask me, and I will do whatever you ask. This is the way the Son will bring honor to the Father. I will do whatever you ask me to do" (John 14:13-14).

"When that time comes, you won't have to ask me about anything. I tell you for certain that the father will give you whatever you ask for in my name. You have not asked for anything in this way before, but now you must ask in my name. Then it will be given to you, so that you will be completely happy" (John 16:23-24).

Jesus encouraged us, *pray for whatever you want, and your prayers will be answered,* according to John 15:7.

He said, *my Father will give you whatever you ask in my name,* according to John 15:16.

A good friend on the 39th day of a 40-day fast was asking for his wife's healing. His sacrifice left him pale and gaunt. His service, love, compassionate concern and physical discipline would surely activate the promises of Christ ... or would it? I mean, if anyone *deserved* a healing, it was this woman whose husband had done all there was to do in the biblical formula: prayers, fasting, faith.

But I don't think there is a formula for healing. I don't think there is an incantation for getting what you want from God. I think that we ask for what we want in the name of Jesus, but we rely on the God we serve to give us what *He* wants for us.

God's promises are true. If we ask and our prayers aren't answered, there must be a problem in the way we are asking, what we are asking for, or perhaps most commonly: *why* we're asking.

In fact, Jesus' promises of answered prayer in John 15 follow a particular word: THEN. This "then" implies that immediately preceding it was a standard that must be reached, a command that must be fulfilled, a condition that must be met.

I have discovered that when we fulfill the IF before the THEN in Jesus' promises, He can answer our prayers and use our obedience to create a spiritual lineage from our works — a lineage that you may never even realize has followed you on this earth.

In Bible days, your lineage was all important: it showed that you knew who your parents, grandparents and distant ancestors were, that you came from good stock, good people.

Our spiritual lineage is equally as important, but much more easy to establish: each Christian has an opportunity (and a responsibility) to begin our own spiritual lineage. That is, the line of Christians who can trace their spiritual heritage back to you. Of course you know who led you to Jesus, whether it was parents, a Sunday School teacher, an evangelist at a crusade, or a combination. I believe in God's great accounting system, each person who contributed to your decision for Christ is credited with that, and you become part of their spiritual lineage.

Then each person you help to bring into the kingdom follows from your own spiritual lineage. I believe, in heaven, you will see each person whose life you impacted, each little bit of fruit you bore for the kingdom, and how the seeds you planted were raised to a spiritual lineage that will amaze you.

That's what this book is all about. Yes, it's about getting your prayers answered, but it is mostly about *why* God answers prayer and the spiritual lineage that will surround you because of answered prayers.

Chapter 1

WHAT ARE YOU ASKING FOR?

'So God granted him what he requested ...'

Many in the church will identify this final refrain from the Jabez prayer of First Chronicles 4, popularized by Bruce Wilkinson's little book, *The Prayer of Jabez*. It's about blessing, or asking for supernatural favor, as Bruce points out, "wanting for ourselves nothing more and nothing less than what God wants for us." The two-verse prayer of an obscure man named Jabez is awakening the church in a way I have rarely experienced in my 18 years of ministry. Bruce's description of the story is this:

- Things started badly for a person no one had ever heard of.
- He prayed an unusual, one-sentence prayer.
- Things ended extraordinarily well.

But did things end extraordinarily well? The Bible confirms that God granted him what he requested, but otherwise we have no record or history of Mr. Jabez. Did he ever lose a loved one to disease or an accident? Did he die young? Did he ever encounter bad times, or was it all good for Jabez? If he had troubles, what was his response?

We assume a life of blessing and expanded territory because that is what he prayed for, and that is what God granted. But what does that mean? Imagine what it means to you in light of your dreams ... and in light of this question: ***what does God want for you?***

Why not take a moment to think about the blessings you have been praying for. Do you find they revolve around success for you and your family, or success for the kingdom of God? Are you praying for physical manifestations of wealth, or spiritual milestones on the way to Christian maturity?

Which was Jabez asking for? (If you haven't read Wilkinson's book, find out more about the Jabez prayer with the link from our ministry website: www.spirituallineage.com.)

These questions are not always easy to answer, although Bruce Wilkinson's book does a masterful job imparting the biblical truths of the Jabez story. The Jabez prayer has had an awesome impact in the Church because it has inspired so many people to pray daily, faithfully believing that God will answer. It illuminates a great truth, and I believe Wilkinson's treatment of that truth is forthright and powerful.

The only drawback is that some folks have selective understanding when reading about Jabez. They internalize only the parts of the story that appeal to them. My father's seat-mate on the plane the other day was reading *The Prayer of Jabez*, and she told Dad she thought it was wonderful because it would help her get more money, a better house, and a better car.

She wasn't a believer, but she expected spiritual principles to apply to her in the physical world. It certainly seems to be working for one church that I heard about which has been experiencing a revival based on the prayer of Jabez. The church has prospered to such an extent that they gave their pastor a 10th anniversary present of a car worth $200,000 and a home worth over $1 million. But I have to wonder: do they get what Jabez is all about?

No doubt it is grand for us as Christians to be blessed with wealth, and I think God likes to bless us because He loves us, and He expects us to invest the resources He gives us in growing His kingdom.

The danger is that mixing up spiritual principles with physical desires can lead us away from what is truly important.

Especially here in America, the popular culture says that physical wealth and worldly power define us. They're what we strive for in the land of the free. But followers of Jesus are supposed to be in this world and not of it. We're supposed to know that ultimately what matters most is what we do for our Lord and Savior.

The prayer of Jabez seems to indicate that it is not wrong for us to ask first and foremost in our prayers for God's blessing on us, and I agree. When we are blessed, we can bless others. Jesus confirmed this in the Lord's prayer, boldly asking for God's blessing of daily provision and forgiveness of debts, as well as for deliverance from evil and victory over temptation.

And of course, Jesus would be the first to say that it is right and fitting to pray for other blessings, such as healing for the sick. He prayed for and healed a multitude of needy people while He walked this earth and continues to miraculously heal today. Praying for blessing is good and right.

But it seems to me that *what* you pray for and *why* you pray for it are as important to whether you get your answer as the method by which you pray. I am thrilled that so many Christians are daily praying the prayer of Jabez and seeing their prayers answered and lives changed.

I would like to submit to this phenomenon that ***it can be even more powerful and pleasing to God when we focus our prayers specifically on what God wants for us***.

What are you praying for ... and why?

I think of a lovely young lady named Natalie from Vladivostok, Russia. I met her when she was 19 years old, studying English at the university in Vladivostok. She was assigned to be my interpreter as I presented the *Book of Hope,* a children's scripture book, in the schools of that city, and as I preached at crusades.

Natalie had been one of the communist party leaders at her university just before the fall of the USSR, and her father was a highly placed communist party official. As she interpreted what I said, I could just feel she didn't like it. She didn't believe in God, and she didn't like having to tell these children that Jesus loved them. That's what I thought, and I knew that she would be the last person to come to Christ.

But then that night at the crusade, Natalie watched as scores of people came forward to accept Christ at the crusade. And later, on a rickety old bus, a homemaker named Anna Gross who was on a short-term missions trip to Russia, was the one to lead Natalie in praying the sinner's prayer and accepting Christ as Savior.

Natalie's whole life changed in an instant, and she came to work with the *Book of Hope* ministry in Russia, during particularly hard times in her country. Eventually she matured into a wonderful Christian lady and married an American missionary.

Now, I don't know what Natalie was praying for specifically, but I know there are millions of Russian girls praying every day for an American green card. They want to marry an American and get out of Russia, because life in Russia is dismal. The Russian Mafia controls the big cities; the rural areas are horribly poor; there's violence, crime, gangs, despair. America is like a dream land for young Russians.

Natalie is married to an American citizen, and she is in the process of becoming a citizen herself. They have been living in the U.S., but just recently I received a call from Natalie and her husband Wayne, and with excitement in their voices, they said, "Rob, we wanted you to be one of the first to know. God has called us to be missionaries."

> You might just say Natalie was going out of the frying pan and into the fire.

I can't disclose their location, but I can say it is predominantly Muslim and, if anything, much worse off economically and much less developed than Russia is. You might just say Natalie was going out of the frying pan and into the fire —

What is she thinking?! Here God gave her the blessed life that is like a dream come true for a Russian girl, and she is rejecting it! What on earth would make a lucky lady like Natalie give up all the blessings of modern American life?

Why, nothing *on earth* possibly could. But Natalie is focused on anything but this earth.

I doubt Natalie was praying, "God, send me to some place where there will be less to eat and fewer conveniences and more danger than Russia." But I know she was praying, "God, send us where we can build your kingdom." And God answered that prayer. Her focus was not on material things and this physical world, but on the spiritual work to which God has called her.

When you ask for what God wants for you, He answers every time.

If you are sure that what you are asking for is what God wants for you, then why hasn't your prayer been answered yet? It could be a simple question of *if* and **THEN**.

Chapter 2

THE *IF* BEFORE
THE *THEN*

Jesus promised to answer my prayers. The Jabez prayer shows that all I have to do is ask.

Right?

Right ... but there's a condition.

In each of the promises of Jesus to answer your every prayer, **there is also a command that must be obeyed before He can honor His promise**.

He said, *"You did not choose me. I chose you and sent you out to produce fruit, the kind of fruit that will last. Then my Father will give you whatever you ask for in my name"* (John 15:16). You bear the fruit, *then* the Father will grant your wish.

"Stay joined to me and let my teachings become part of you. Then you can pray for whatever you want, and your prayer will be answered" (John 15:7). If you remain in me, *then* you receive what you ask for.

"I tell you for certain that if you have faith in me, you will do

the same things that I am doing. You will do even greater things, now that I am going back to the Father. Ask me, and I will do whatever you ask. This way the Son will bring honor to the Father" (John 14:12-13). You have faith in me, and *then* I will give you what you ask in my name.

Bear the fruit that He has commanded you to bear, and *then* ... He will grant whatever you ask.

If you want to receive the desires of your heart, if you want the Jabez blessings, then you must first do the work of the kingdom that Jesus has appointed for you. You must first bear the fruit that He has commanded you to bear, and *then* ... He will grant whatever you ask in His name.

Jesus' words make it clear that in order to activate the promises, you must first do something. So what exactly does Jesus want us to do in order to receive the fulfillment of His promises?

Seven times in John 14-16, Jesus encourages us: "Obey my commands." Obviously the first positive action we can take is to obey the commands of the Savior. In fact, Jesus equates our willingness to obey His commands with our love for Him.

- John 14:15, If you love me, you will do as I command.
- John 14:21, If you love me, you will do what I have said, and my Father will love you. I will also love you and show you what I am like.
- John 14:23, If anyone loves me, they will obey me. Then my Father will love them, and we will come to them and live in them
- John 15:10, If you obey me, I will keep loving you, just

as my Father keeps loving me, because I have obeyed Him.
* John 15:14,   And you are my friends, if you obey me.

Clearly, the Lord means for us to obey His commands, and as Christians, we are anxious to do so. What are these commands?

The first is to love one another. Jesus says, *"Now I tell you to love each other as I have loved you"* (John 15:12) and, *"I have loved you, just as my Father has loved me. So remain faithful in my love for you"* (John 15:9).

The result of our Christian love for one another as believers is to be a unity of the spirit, the second command of Christ in this passage: be one.

And finally, there is this command: ***bear fruit.***

Jesus said:

> *I am the true vine, and my Father is the gardener. He cuts away every branch of mine that doesn't produce fruit. But He trims clean every branch that does produce fruit, so that it will produce even more fruit. You are already clean because of what I have said to you.*
>
> *Stay joined to me, and I will stay joined to you. Just as a branch cannot produce fruit unless it stays joined to the vine, you cannot produce fruit unless you stay joined to me. I am the vine, and you are the branches. If you stay joined to me, and I stay joined to you, then you will produce lots of fruit. If you don't stay joined to me, you will be thrown away. You will be like dry branches that are gathered up and burned in a fire.*

Stay joined to me and let my teachings become part of you. Then you can pray for whatever you want, and your prayer will be answered. When you become fruitful disciples of mine, my Father will be honored.

John 15:1-8

And here we come to the important work of the kingdom: **to bear fruit, much fruit, fruit that will last**. When we find ourselves engaged in this work, then there is no end to the prayers and petitions that Jesus will grant for us, for we have complied with the command which comes before *"Then* my Father will give you whatever you for ask in my name" of John 15:16.

When Jesus says to bear fruit for the kingdom of God, what is He talking about? What is the only thing we can take into the kingdom with us, the only thing that will last? It is the souls of those who hear and respond to the message of salvation because of us. It is the spiritual lineage we build for ourselves once we come to Christ.

This is the fruit that will last.

I think of Anya, a little six-year-old girl in Izhevsk, Russia, back in 1998. She received our *Book of Hope*, the children's Scripture book, and then she started asking some Christian children she knew questions about Jesus. They invited her to church with them, and little Anya made a decision to follow Christ. She brought her older brother to church, and he made a commitment to Jesus, too.

Their grandma, Rimma, had been to the Russian Orthodox Church, and she always asked Anya about her church, "How can you pray? You have no candles and no icons. What kind of church is that?"

But Anya said, "Grandma, God is everywhere. You can pray to Him any time, anywhere. He is alive! My book tells me this. You will have to come to church and see for yourself."

So Grandma Rimma came to church, and she accepted Christ as Savior. Then Anya's mom, Natasha became a Christian.

Rimma sent the *Book of Hope* to her son Vladimir, who was in prison. He wrote back to her, "Mother, thank you for the book. It changed my life. It was as if I were learning from the ABC book. It opened my eyes! I want to start my life over."

Today, Vladimir is taking correspondence Bible courses to become a minister. Anya is nine years old now, and we just recently received a report that she had taken another stack of *Books of Hope* to school with her, to evangelize her friends and classmates.

She and her whole family, except for her father, are joyfully serving Jesus. And we are praying that her dad will soon come into relationship with Jesus, too. Please pray with us. (For more exciting testimonies of God's word changing hearts and lives, visit our ministry website: www.spirituallineage.com.)

Little Anya already has a wonderful spiritual lineage. She has already brought her whole family to Jesus. **She is already bearing fruit for the kingdom, fruit that will last.**

It is only by bearing fruit for the kingdom that we raise up for ourselves the spiritual lineage that God wants for us.

When we are bearing fruit, then we are open to blessing. In fact, the blessings of the Jabez prayer are only guaranteed to you when you are bearing the fruit God has appointed for you. Jesus Himself gave what can be seen as a messianic confirmation of the Jabez prayer in His instructions in the book of John.

Chapter 3

How Jesus Confirmed the Jabez Prayer

Let's compare the three parts of the Jabez prayer with the assertions that Jesus made in John 14-16. Says Jabez:

"Oh, that you would bless me indeed, and enlarge my territory, that your hand would be with me, and that you would keep me from evil, that I may not cause pain!"

1 Chronicles 4:10, NIV

1. "Oh that you would bless me indeed ..."

Jesus' Words of John 14:13-14 speak of remarkable blessing: *"And I will do whatever you ask in my name, so that the Son may bring glory to the Father. You may ask me for anything in my name, and I will do it"* (NIV).

Again in John 16:23-24, Jesus promises, *"In that day you will no longer ask me anything. I tell you the truth, my Father will give you whatever you ask in my name. Until now you have not asked for anything in my name. Ask and you will receive, and your joy will*

29

be complete" (NIV).

Apparently our heavenly Father does want to bless us indeed, just as Jabez suspected — and here we have Christ's confirmation of it.

2. "And enlarge my territory ..."

Jesus confirms His desire to enlarge your territory with His promises of John 15:5 and 15:16 ...*"If you stay joined to me, and I stay joined to you, then you will produce lots of fruit"* and *"You did not choose me. I chose you and sent you out to produce fruit, the kind of fruit that will last ..."*

"Fruit that will last" has become such a real concept to me in the past few years because of the work of the *Book of Hope*. Certainly when we first began giving this children's scripture book to kids in the schools around the world, we saw that it would bear fruit.

Children were drawn to the book, and when we presented it in conjunction with evangelistic crusades, we often saw remarkable numbers of children and youth turning to Jesus. But we had our detractors, too. Some people said literature evangelism and crusades were just "hit-and-run," and we would not really make a difference.

But we have seen fruit that lasts.

It has now been nearly 10 years since the *Book of Hope* was first given to the children of Krasnoyarsk, Russia. Olga was one of the first kids who received the book in her classroom at school, and it meant so much to her. She had such a bad birth defect, she could barely get around where she wanted to go with a cane. The other kids were cruel, and they had teased her a lot because of her handicap. She was lonely and sad.

Then she met Jesus in the pages of the *Book of Hope*. She prayed with the members of the American volunteer team that brought the book to her school, and she dedicated her heart and life to Christ. She was filled with such joy and hope for the future! Today, Olga is a beautiful young lady who serves as a missionary to Uzbekistan, and also as an interpreter for Book of Hope teams in Russia.

Fruit that will last! When we abide in Jesus, and His words abide in us, then He gives us fruit that will last for the kingdom of God. I could tell you hundreds of real stories like that off the top of my head. One of the churches that our ministry helped to plant in Siberia in 1992 is about to commission its first missionary to China. Dima, this bright star on the missions horizon to a nation hungry for hope, had also received the *Book of Hope* in school, back in 1992, and committed his life to Christ because of it.

Jesus does want to enlarge our territory — **by allowing us to bear fruit that LASTS for the kingdom.**

3. "That your hand would be with me, and that you would keep me from evil ..."

Again and again, Jesus promised that He would be with us: *"Stay joined to me, and I will stay joined to you"* (John 15:4) and *"If you stay joined to me, and I stay joined to you, then you will produce lots of fruit"* (John 15:5).

But keep in mind that His presence with us seems to be predicated upon our willingness to obey His commands, for He said, *"I have loved you, just as my Father has loved me. So remain faithful to my love for you. If you obey me, I will keep loving you"* (John 15:9-10).

Jesus has promised His hand with us — **especially when we are obedient to His commands.**

Now you have seen that the Prayer of Jabez, which the Bible says God honored when Jabez prayed it, does indeed have confirmation in the New Testament, from the very lips of the Savior. The key to receiving your Jabez blessings lies in:

- **understanding the intent of the promises and**
- **obeying the commands Christ gave.**

I don't believe the prayer of Jabez and the promises of Jesus were intended to operate as physical principles in this material world. They weren't intended to line your pockets or get you a bigger house or car. They are spiritual principles that can be correctly applied when we concern ourselves with doing the business of God's kingdom.

Take Olga, for instance. When we first spoke about Jesus in her classroom when she was just a young teenager, her teacher originally asked us to pray for Olga's *physical healing*. As far as her teacher could tell, that was Olga's principal need. Although Olga did not receive physical healing at that moment, she says a much greater work was accomplished, for she felt God's love for her and determined to accept Christ as Savior.

Today, Olga still awaits physical healing. If anyone's heart and motives are pure and right before God, it is Olga. So why has God chosen not to heal her, after all these years? Why isn't the promise "ask what you will" true for Olga? Olga says her prayers have been answered: God is using her to win souls to His kingdom. Although she still walks on a crutch, she bears fruit for the kingdom in ways that many of us who are physically whole have never even attempted.

Olga says God has blessed her indeed in the spiritual realm, which is vastly more important than the physical.

If we insist on applying spiritual principles to our physical circumstances, then it merely proves that we do not know our Father's heart business very well.

The scripture that God has impressed on my heart as my life verse is Second Corinthians 4:17-18 (NIV):

Olga says her prayers have been answered: God is using her to win souls.

"For our light and momentary troubles are achieving for us an eternal glory that far outweighs them all. So we fix our eyes not on what is seen, but on what is unseen. For what is seen is temporary, but what is unseen is eternal."

If we fix our eyes only on what we can see, then we have fixed our focus on the least important thing of all. The spiritual is the eternal, not the physical. And for this, the eternal, the spiritual, we have been given the promises of Jesus and the prayer of Jabez.

If we try to use those promises and that prayer for any other purpose or in any other way, it just won't work — and we will be frustrated and confused.

However, I promise you that when applied to the spiritual kingdom, the principles of John 15 work. The pages of this small book cannot contain all the confirmation stories I have experienced in my life in ministry since I have begun applying these principles, but I will share one recent experience with you.

Not long ago, I opened a copy of the *USA Today* newspaper and read about a small, West African nation called Benin. What caught my eye was that an African nation was cited as the world capital of Voodooism, basically a nation of witchcraft.

I laid down the paper and began to pray: "Lord, you said to ask for anything (bless me indeed) and you said to bear much fruit that will last (expand my territory). You said to be obedient, so Lord I ask you for this spiritually desolate nation. I ask you for much fruit, for many souls in this nation. And as always Lord, keep my heart and my motives pure."

As I prayed, I felt a holy chill run through my body.

I'd like to say I'm not surprised anymore when God responds so quickly and so miraculously to such a simple prayer, but I'd be lying. I wasn't prepared to receive God's response as soon as I did.

The very next day after I prayed that prayer, an old missionary friend of mine called. "Rob," he said, "I have a favor to ask. Christie and the girls and I are changing fields. We're going to Benin in West Africa, and I would like you to pray about helping us get the *Book of Hope* to every schoolchild in the country."

Over and over, God has answered my prayers when I have prayed for the fruit He wants me to bring into the kingdom. But by the same token, I have heard of Christians in tough mission fields who never reap the harvest, no matter how hard they pray. So why aren't their prayers working? Let's take a look at that question in the next chapter.

~ Chapter 4 ~

WHY DOESN'T
IT WORK?

If God is honor-bound to answer our prayers when we pray for what He wants for us, why doesn't the prayer of Jabez work?

Why did the disciples of Christ, the devout men to whom the promises of Jesus were first given, end their lives in prison or in martyrdom?

Or why does a dedicated missionary like Adoniram Judson die in poverty and obscurity, having made only a handful of converts in all his years of service?

His story is bleak: in 1813, Adoniram Judson became the first American missionary to foreign shores. He and his wife Ann had planned to work for the Lord in India, but found themselves so endlessly persecuted, rejected and driven away from India that they were forced to take up residence in nearby Burma, the nation today called Myanmar. Here Judson felt God's calling to evangelize the Buddhist people of Burma.

The going was far from easy: at the hands of their despotic emperor, converts could face confiscation of property, imprisonment, torture, even death. It was six years before Judson baptized even his first convert. During that time, his wife's health began to deteriorate, and then their eight-month-old baby died.

Judson knew he needed help and tried to sail to the village of Chittagong, where he heard that British missionaries had started a church. He determined to invite some of the Burmese Christians back with him, to help in the work. The sailing, which should have taken three months, went horribly wrong, and Judson returned alone, nearly nine months later.

By 1822, nine years after their arrival in Burma, Judson had managed to raise a church of ten members. The high point of church membership for all his years of service in Burma was to be 18, but this rapidly diminished in 1824, when war broke out between England and India/Burma, and Judson was arrested and imprisoned along with other westerners living in Burma.

For 21 months, he lived a hellish existence in a crowded and filthy Burmese prison. His ankles were weighted with five pairs of leg irons all day. Every night, his jailers would tie his arms and legs to a bamboo pole, then raise his arms above his legs and leave him hanging from the pole like that, all night long. That is how he slept every night in prison.

Imagine his horror when his wife visited with their infant daughter, who was born shortly after Judson was arrested. They brought him food in this hideous place, and saw the terrible conditions to which he had been reduced.

Then he heard that small pox had stricken his family. Both his wife and little girl were nearly killed by the disease. His wife's health was frail to begin with — shortly before Judson was imprisoned, Ann had been forced to leave for more than two years in order to recover her health in America. Judson must have been worried that she would die while he suffered in prison. Who would take care of their baby?

At age 36, he was finally released from prison, and found his church reduced to just four Burmese Christians. The same year he was set free, his wife died. The following year, his little daughter Maria died at just two years and seven months old.

Now Judson had buried both his children and his beloved wife in the foreign soil of Burma. He had managed, in 14 years of missions work, to win and keep only four converts to Christianity.

I don't imagine Adoniram Judson felt blessed.

It doesn't sound like he was blessed. In fact, **it sounds like he was cursed!**

Yet he had done his very best to honor God. He spent hours each day in prayer. He dedicated himself to winning souls in Burma. And God didn't expand his territory. God did not bless him with wealth and leisure. God did not keep him from evil.

God allowed him to be thrown into prison and tortured, and God allowed his family to weaken and die. Judson labored the rest of his life in Burma. He said he would stay with his mission until he had raised the cross of Christ over Burma. He repeatedly attempted to penetrate Central Burma and preach the Gospel to the majority population who lived there, and he

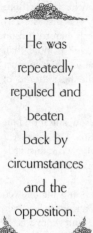

He was repeatedly repulsed and beaten back by circumstances and the opposition.

was repeatedly repulsed and beaten back by circumstances and the opposition of the Buddhists in control of the country.

He eventually died in Burma, having led only a tiny flock of Burmese people to Jesus.

Is our God so cruel that He denied Adoniram Judson the sweet taste of victory in Jesus simply because Adoniram failed to ask for what he wanted according to the Jabez prayer? It can't be. I'm sure that Adoniram Judson prayed daily for the people of Burma and for God's blessing on his ministry. So why was it such a dreadful failure?

Why didn't his prayers *work*?

If we believe the prayer of Jabez and the promises of Christ, we must believe that it is next to impossible for a committed Christian to have a less than successful life, right? Yet even the apostle Peter suffered a horrible end: he was crucified upside-down. It does not sound as if things ended extraordinarily well for him, either. Here was a man who deserved Jabez blessings if there ever was one: once he recognized the lordship of Jesus Christ, he spent the rest of his life spreading the Gospel, even when it meant great risk and physical deprivation for him.

So what happened? Why didn't Jesus pour out Jabez blessings on Peter, His rock? Why didn't Jesus bless the selfless efforts of Adoniram Judson?

Guess what?

Their prayers *did* work.

God did give them the promised blessings of His word — just not in the way we might think the Jabez prayer ought to work. As Bruce Wilkinson points out in his book, the prayer is not designed to deliver personal wealth to you, but rather to expand your territory for the kingdom of God.

It is spiritual, not physical.

What does that mean? What is the expanded territory of God's kingdom? According to Jesus, it is fruit, the fruit of ministry, the harvest of souls. In that area, every prayer of Peter was answered, for the Gospel he preached has been carried through his spiritual lineage to nearly the entire world. Can you imagine Peter's spiritual family tree?

However 2,000 years later there are still two billion plus who have never once heard the Gospel. Could it be that God is calling you to add them to *your* spiritual lineage?

Oh, as it turns out, the prayers of Adoniram Judson were answered, too. I can attest to that by telling you about my father's recent visit to Burma.

Chapter 5

It Did Work!

My dad is a great missionary and evangelist, in addition to being an author, a gospel publisher, and founder of the Book of Hope ministry. He once preached a powerful evangelistic crusade in Burma, back in 1962. His interpreter for that crusade was a young aeronautical engineer named Myo Chit, and he was one of the finest interpreters Dad had ever worked with. When my dad made a gesture, Myo copied the gesture in his interpretation. When my dad used a certain facial expression, Myo simulated it exactly. His pacing, tone, inflection — everything he interpreted for the people was as close to what my father said and intended as anyone could possibly get.

For a missionary, Myo Chit was a dream interpreter, the one we always hope to have! But from a ministry standpoint, it was obvious to my dad that Myo didn't need to interpret for foreigners — he needed to preach! He could be a fabulous evangelist in his own right, and my dad told him so. "You have been called," Dad told him. "You would be a great preacher."

"No," Myo said. "I am an aeronautical engineer, not a preacher."

Not long after my father left Burma, the governmental systems changed, and all the foreign missionaries were expelled. The young Burmese church looked anxiously for leadership, and

They turned
to an
intelligent
young
Christian
man who
had all the
earmarks
of a great
Christian
leader.

they turned to an intelligent young Christian man who had all the earmarks of a great Christian leader, Myo Chit.

My father returned to Burma in 2001, to find Myo Chit as the Superintendent of the Assemblies of God, overseeing 1,000 thriving churches and at the helm of a powerful Christian movement in the country now known as Myanmar. As he and my father renewed their acquaintance, my dad marveled at how greatly God had used Myo since the last time they had spoken, and Myo happened to mention his own spiritual lineage:

His great-great-grandfather was the second convert of Adoniram Judson.

The missionary who vowed he would not leave Burma until he had raised the cross of Christ over that nation had indeed accomplished his aim: just four generations after he began it. Although he did not see the fruit of his labor while physically present on this earth, his efforts to win a tiny handful of people to Jesus have resulted in a huge evangelical movement in Burma!

Adoniram's ministry was blessed indeed. God expanded his territory in ways greater than he could ever have imagined. He received his blessing and the answers to his prayers, in God's good timing. Myo Chit, whose great-great-grandfather was among Judson's first converts, is part of the spiritual lineage of Adoniram Judson. Further, those who come to Christ through Myo Chit's efforts will also be of the same spiritual lineage begun by the obedience of Adoniram Judson.

Years ago, I was on a seven-hour flight from Siberia to Moscow, and I was perfectly exhausted from all the ministry work I had done, counting on catching the flight home from Moscow to see my wife and daughter again.

The Russian gentleman next to me on the plane spoke English. He had a newspaper, so I asked him what was in the news. This was before the fall of the old USSR — Gorbachev was still in power, but things were really stirred up: there were riots, strikes, a financial crisis and a great move toward throwing off the chains of communism. These were exciting times!

My seat-mate on the plane began to tell me that at that moment in the Siberian town of Kamerovo, the coal miners were on strike. Up until very recently, the idea of a strike was unheard of in Russia, and because of the importance of the coal industry in Kamerovo, this strike was getting a lot of attention. In fact, it was about to touch off what would become known as the "Second Russian Revolution," which brought down the USSR.

As we talked, I began to hear the Lord's leading, and he was saying, "Kamerovo. Go to Kamerovo." Nothing could have been lower on my wish list than to go to Kamerovo. It was back in Siberia, in the complete opposite direction from where I wanted to go. I told the Lord, "I want to see my wife and daughter. I've been gone too much as it is." But the only reply I received was this: *Kamerovo.*

> Nothing could have been lower on my wish list than to go to Kamerovo.

When the plane landed in Moscow, a Russian pastor had come to meet me and help me get from the domestic airport to the international airport for my flight home. He was dumbfounded when I asked, "Can I get to Kamerovo from here tonight?"

He said, "Kamerovo is in Siberia. You just came from Siberia."

I said, "I know it sounds crazy, but the Lord has told me to go to Kamerovo."

We found out there was only one flight to Kamerovo that night, and it was oversold. I was so happy! There was no way myself and my interpreter could get on an oversold flight. Just so God could see I was trying to be obedient, I put our names on the standby list, knowing that we would never be able to go ... until at the last moment, *one* seat cleared.

If I went, I would go alone, with no interpreter, to a Russian city I'd never been to, hours in the wrong direction from the one place I wanted to be.

I went. I wasn't happy about it, but I went.

About six o'clock the next morning, I arrived in Kamerovo, a city of 700,000 people, where I knew not a soul, a city in chaos because of the labor strikes, where I could only communicate through hand gestures. If you know anything about the Russian language, you know there's no such thing as knowing "enough Russian to get by." I managed to get to a hotel, drop to my knees before God and say, "I'm here with no idea what I'm doing here. Now what?"

After I prayed and interceded for the city of Kamerovo, I thought maybe that was all I had to do — pray. Maybe God had called me here just to pray for Kamerovo. But then God spoke to me again, to go to the university, and find someone who speaks English. God led me to a student named Julie who wanted to practice her English. She took me to see the mayor of Kamerovo. Three months later, I came back to that city with a team of ministry volunteers and the *Book of Hope* for every student in the city.

During that ministry event, 16,000 boys and girls signed decision cards saying they wanted to follow Jesus. We were able to leave a great missionary couple in Kamerovo to begin a new church, and a wonderful work was born.

Not long ago, I met a young man from Kamerovo named Ilia. He said he wanted to thank me for bringing the *Book of Hope*, because the book led him to the Lord eight years ago when he received it in school.

He said, "I don't know if you know what has been happening with the church in Kamerovo since then. A bunch of us at the university realized nobody had taken the *Book of Hope* to the city of Nobokutzneks, so we did a distribution there, and we helped a church plant which has about 800 members now."

Further, he told me, the believers at Nobokutzneks were worried about the Altea people in the mountains beyond them, because they had never heard of Jesus. So these new believers in Nobokutzneks took the *Book of Hope* to the Altea people.

If you look them up, they are listed among the "most unreached people groups" of the world. But that is going to have to change, because there are now 36 Christians among those

Buddhist Alteas!

Today, there is a thriving church in the city of
Kamerovo, a church in Nobokutzneks, and 36 believers
among the Altea — and I believe in some ways God credits
those as my spiritual lineage ... because I trusted in Him, gave
up my own comfort and my own desires, and followed God's
leading back to Siberia. And I should say in turn, that they are
also part of the spiritual lineage of all those who support me
(from my wife and daughters to those who pray and give finan-
cially to keep me on the mission field).

Even if what God asks you to do seems difficult and con-
trary to your own common sense, He can use your obedience to
raise up a legacy to your faithfulness and His ability to answer
your prayers.

The life of the apostle Peter is a perfect example of what I
am talking about. It seemed to Peter that Jesus' plans for lordship were nonsensical — especially when He began talking
about being delivered to the authorities and killed! Peter was
destined to fail miserably in that moment of crisis. Yet when he
finally got the right vision of who Jesus was, God blessed his
ministry and raised his spiritual lineage in remarkable ways.

Let me explain how Peter's vision of Jesus changed
everything.

Chapter 6

THE RIGHT VISION OF JESUS

Our lives, dreams and desires can be transformed once we get the right vision of Jesus, understand who He is, and what His message is. In John 13, Peter makes it clear that he has not yet realized who Jesus is, or what His purpose on this earth is.

The disciples were convinced of the Judaic idea that the Messiah would come in power to rule the earth in a physical kingdom. They had flocked to Jesus with the impression that He would become the ruler of this physical world. At His right and left hands, they supposed they would be blessed with physical wealth. This is what their tradition taught them, and this is what they expected.

When Christ spoke of His coming death and resurrection, He told the disciples that where He was about to go, they could not follow. "Why not?" Peter demands. "I am ready to lay down my life for you." Not only did Peter not realize who Jesus was and what His program was, Peter did not even know himself very well.

"Would you really die for me? Jesus asked. I tell you for certain that before a rooster crows, you will say three times that you

don't even know me" (John 13:38). Jesus' thoughts must have been heavy ... *Peter, you don't even know who I am. You have an historical idea of what I am going to do for you, and it is about 180 degrees opposite of what is actually going to happen.*

If we insist on misinterpreting scriptures like the Jabez prayer as promises of financial wealth and physical comfort, then we have made the same mistake as Peter. We have confused the spiritual with the physical ... and remember, it is only the spiritual that lasts, only the spiritual that is eternal.

> We have
> confused the
> spiritual
> with the
> physical.

In John 14, Thomas then spoke for all the disciples — including Peter — when he inquired, "Lord, we don't know where you are going, so how can we know the way?" And Philip demanded "Show us the father, and then we'll be satisfied." All these months they had sat at the feet of the Master, and it was as if they had heard nothing that He preached and seen nothing of His miracles.

Sometimes we Christians are too willing to follow in the same mindset as the seemingly blind disciples. **We have an idea of what Jesus is going to do for us in this physical world, and we are loath to let go of that and face the reality of who Jesus is.**

He said in explanation to Thomas:

"I am the way and the truth and the life. No one comes to the Father except through me. If you really knew me, you would know my Father as well" (John 14:6-7).

This statement of absolute truth, of only one way to salvation, flies in the face of everything our relativistic modern culture teaches. We want a Jesus who is very tolerant and open to saving the souls of all "good" people, whether or not they have ever confessed Christ as Savior. But Jesus' statement here, and biblical mandates throughout the New Testament, make it clear that is not the case.

Could it be we have the wrong idea of who Jesus is and what His mission is, just as Peter and the disciples originally did? Perhaps the overwhelming response to the prayer of Jabez even bears witness to this possibility, for to some Christians it speaks to their desires for a physical kingdom, a blessing indeed, upon their own lives — without regard to what the purpose of their lives in Christ ought to be.

But we cannot continue in this fantasy if we want to be useful in the kingdom of God. Jesus' prophetic words over Peter proved true. In the moment of crisis, he denied the Lord three times. In that moment of utter horror and anguish, Peter was forced to face the fact that he had been quite mistaken about who Jesus was and what His purpose was. Obviously if He could be put to death by the human authorities on this earth, He was not going to establish a physical kingdom in the here and now of Peter's day.

What then?

Peter was in turmoil. He was frightened out of his wits. He had placed his faith in a kingdom to come that was *not* to come in his lifetime. He had failed the Lord he loved in fear for his own life, and felt disgraced and hopeless — as well as still endangered by the authorities who could come after the followers of Christ.

Yet that picture is completely different from the Peter we see in the last chapter of John. The resurrection has not only transformed the risen Savior, but it has transformed His disciples as well. In John 21, we find them out on the Sea of Tiberius, having fished all night and caught nothing.

A stranger on the shore gives them some advice about which side of the boat to cast their nets from, and suddenly they are bringing in a huge amount of fish. John leans over to Peter and points to the stranger on the shore. He whispers in Peter's ear, "It is the Lord."

All of a sudden, Peter leaps out of the boat! He totally abandons himself to the joy of being reunited with the Savior. He has no fears and no worries about who sees him with Jesus. He will never again deny the Lord. **Peter, swimming for the shore with all his might, is a picture of abandonment to the will of God, abandonment to the Savior's plan.**

They breakfasted together on the sea shore, then the Bible says:

> When Jesus and His disciples had finished eating, He asked, "Simon, son of John, do you love me more than the others do?"
>
> Simon Peter answered, "Yes, Lord, you know I do!"
>
> Jesus asked a second time, "Simon, son of John, do you love me?"
>
> Peter answered, "Yes, Lord, you know I love you!"

"Then take care of my sheep," Jesus told him. Jesus asked a third time, "Simon, son of John, do you love me?"

Peter was hurt because Jesus had asked him three times if he loved him. So he told Jesus, "Lord, you know everything. You know I love you."

Jesus replied, "Feed my sheep. I tell you for certain that when you were a young man, you dressed yourself and went wherever you wanted to go. But when you are old, you will hold out your hands. Then others will wrap your belt around you and lead you where you don't want to go."

Jesus said this to tell how Peter would die and bring honor to God. Then He said to Peter, "Follow me!"

John 21:15-19

Jesus clearly gives Peter instructions for his new mission in life: to win souls and disciples into the kingdom. If Peter loves the Lord, that is his only option. But then the Lord adds something more to these instructions — a prophecy of the death Peter will die. He will be led where he does not want to go, martyred for the cause of Christ.

At this moment, there is no hesitation. Peter does not balk at being told that in his old age he will be mercilessly killed for preaching the Gospel. He has abandoned all notions of what he thought his life ought to be and what he thought Jesus ought to do for him and is clearly ready to follow Jesus, come what may.

This is the total abandonment that Jesus is looking for in His followers today. He does not want us to remain willfully blinded by the idea of a physical kingdom of our own, or a

He does not
want us to
remain willfully
blinded by
the idea of
a physical
kingdom of
our own.

politically correct Jesus who will save everyone regardless of whether or not they have believed on Him.

When we are abandoned to Him and dedicated to bearing fruit for His kingdom, then He can use us, and He will provide for us. I think of Adoniram Judson at the end of his days. He was so ill and wasted from a life of deprivation and harsh climates, his doctors had prescribed an ocean voyage to restore his health and spirits.

Because of various unavoidable delays, the ship he had boarded did not commence out to sea for several days. During this time, Judson's body continued to weaken, and by the time the ship finally sailed, he was nearing death — and he knew it. After years of struggle and defeat in Burma, his benediction on his death bed was this:

"I suppose they think me an old man, and imagine it is nothing for one like me to resign a life so full of trials. But I am not old — at least in that sense; you know I am not. Oh, no man ever left the world with more inviting prospects, with brighter hopes, or warmer feelings — warmer feelings."

He did not know at the moment of his death that he had planted the seeds for the Gospel to spread throughout Burma. He did not know that his spiritual lineage would raise up Myo Chit, a powerful evangelist and preacher to lead the Burmese church through some of its darkest hours. But he knew that God had used him, and that whether he lived or died, it would all be to the glory of God.

How could material possessions or physical wealth even compare with that hope of glory at the end of life?

The "bless me indeed" of Jabez would be *cheap indeed* if it amounted only to money or things.

But the blessing of a life well lived in the cause of Christ and a legacy of fruit that will last for the kingdom — that is a spiritual treasure you take with you from this life, into the next.

Chapter 7

WALKING
HIS TRAIL

One of my closest friends, Mart Green, felt led to make a motion picture about the five American missionaries who died on their mission to reach a prehistoric tribe in Ecuador. (For more information on this film, check out the link at our ministry website: www.spirituallineage.com.) In Christian circles, the story of these five brave families, who gave up so much so that an obscure people would hear about Jesus, is well known.

What most of us don't know is that after the five were martyred, Jim Elliot's wife Elizabeth Elliot and Nate Saint's sister Rachel Saint went back and remained in Ecuador to carry on the work of their loved ones. In fact, Rachel lived there for a number of years, until she died in 1994. Her nephew, and Nate's son, Steve Saint was asked by the tribe to come for Rachel's burial service in the jungle.

While he was there, the tribe asked him to come and take his aunt's place, ministering to the tribe fulltime. Steve was a successful businessman who had really achieved the American dream and had a beautiful wife and family. The idea of abandoning their life in the U.S. seemed ludicrous at first, but as he and his wife Ginny prayed, they felt that it was actually God's will for them.

They moved with their four children from the comfort of their lives to one of the most primitive spots on the planet. Their testimony is a wonderful story of reconciliation. The man who had actually killed Steve's father found Christ as Savior. "We used to act badly, badly," he said, "until we learned His carvings, and now we walk His trail."

In August of 2000, my friend Mart, who was making the motion picture about the martyrs, knew that I would be at a Billy Graham conference for ministers and missionaries in Amsterdam. While there, he asked if I would like to meet this missionary, Steve Saint, and Mincaye, a member of the killing party that had once upon a time murdered Steve's dad.

> It was one of the most spiritually significant moments of my life to meet two men from two different worlds.

I would have to say it was one of the most spiritually significant moments of my life to meet two men from two different worlds. In the physical realm, they should have been filled with loathing and anger for one another ... but because of the message of the cross, they had not only been reconciled but had developed a supernatural love for one another.

In fact, Steve's children had grown up calling this once savage killer "grandfather."

The saddest part of this meeting was the knowledge that just weeks before we met in

Amsterdam, Steve and his wife Ginny had lost their 20-year-old daughter Stephenie. She had just returned from a year-long missions trip. Naturally she was exhausted and told her mother she wanted to lie down for a little while. She just never woke up.

I could not even imagine losing one of my daughters. To be honest, I did not know what words of comfort I could possibly say to Steve as I was meeting him for the first time. I believe God's Word when it says He will not give any of us more than we can bear. But looking at the tragedy of Steve's life — losing his father when he was still young, then losing a daughter while *she* was still young — I don't know how a person bears that.

Like Adoniram Judson, **he had given his all to the cause of Christ, only to see his own hopes and dreams for his precious child die with her before she was even 21 years old**.

I really wanted to honor both Steve and Mincaye that day, so I chose one of the nicest restaurants in Amsterdam. It was on a beautiful lake and packed with affluent European business-men. I had asked my good friend Stephan Tchividjian to join us.

For a few moments, the whole experience seemed surreal, like something out of that movie you may have seen called *The God's Must Be Crazy.*

Mincaye was venturing out of the jungle for one of the first times in his life, and you could tell he was finding everything in our "sophisticated" culture rather comical.

He found it especially humorous when our stuffy waiters delivered a palate-teaser to the table: a smoked herring about half an inch long. When Mincaye found out how much I was paying for that bite of fish, he was even more amused: it would have fed his village for a year!

If I have ever seen a living demonstration of the unseen confronting the seen world, it was there.

Steve asked Mincaye to pray before our meal, and if I have ever seen a living demonstration of the unseen confronting the seen world, it was there in that dining room in Holland. As Mincaye prayed in his tribal tongue and Steve translated, I felt an overwhelming presence of God's Spirit descend upon us.

Mincaye prayed a rather loud and lengthy prayer. He gave thanks to God for his salvation and all of ours. He talked about the cross and the sacrifice of Christ. He named tribal member after tribal member who had come to the Lord.

He began to talk about heaven in a way that I have heard few believers ever describe it, and then spoke about "Nemo Star," the tribal name for Stephenie, Steve's daughter who had just died weeks before. He poured out his heart to God about how much he missed Stephenie, but how glad he was that because he was an old man, **he would soon be joining her in heaven, and how he looked forward to that day.**

As Steve translated this, with a tremor in his voice, I am sure he envisioned his daughter. And I was once again confronted with the awesome power of eternity, and the mere finiteness of our lives here on earth.

With Mincaye's final "Amen," I opened my tear-filled eyes ...

and I saw that many of the businessmen had set down their knives and forks and were looking at this little, primitive tribesman with the presence of someone who knew more than they did.

I looked at Stephan, with tears on his cheeks, and I thought of the rich spiritual heritage both of us come from — I'm sure he felt the same way I did at that moment. *Lord, teach me to trust you as deeply as these men do.*

That night Steve and Mincaye shared with the approximately 12,000 people at the Billy Graham conference, Steve asked all the people who had been impacted by the death of his father and the other four missionaries in Ecuador to stand. I would say 90% of those evangelists and ministers from more than 200 countries stood to express their thanks and appreciation for those five men and their families.

Their reward will be incalculable until that day when they stand before the Savior, and He says, "Well done, my good and faithful servants."

Their prayers for the tribe they were called to serve are being answered, and the spiritual lineage of them and their surviving family members and children continues to grow. Steve and Ginny Saint are now directing I-Tech Ministries, an organization that leverages technology and innovation to help indigenous churches reach their world with the Gospel. (For more information on I-Tech, check out the link from our website: www.spirituallineage.com.)

Jesus calls each one of us to follow Him and bear fruit for His kingdom. The path He chooses for us may not always be the one we would have chosen for ourselves, but this is where faith comes into play. He does not ask us to understand His ways, merely to abide in them. He said:

"If you remain in me and my words remain in you, ask whatever you wish, and it will be given you" (John 15:7, NIV). Mincaye might say it this way: "We used to act badly, badly, until we learned His carvings, and now we walk His trail." It may not always be easy to walk in his trail, but it is always right and always fulfilling.

Because Jesus is your friend, and He has appointed you to do the most worthwhile work in the universe.

Chapter 8

HE CALLS YOU
FRIEND

Before His death, Jesus told the disciples:

> *The greatest way to show love for friends is to die for them. And you are my friends, if you obey me. Servants don't know what their master is doing, and so I don't speak to you as my servants. I speak to you as my friends, and I have told you everything that my Father has told me.*
>
> **You did not choose me. I chose you and sent you out to produce fruit, the kind of fruit that lasts. Then my Father will give you whatever you ask for in my name.**
>
> *John 15:13-16*

At that moment, there was a great shift in the relationship between Christ and His followers. At that point, Jesus made the great distinction between servants and friends, and He called those of us who follow Him His friends. How do we attain this friendship with Jesus? By understanding the business of the Father.

A son does not reveal the family business to servants, as Jesus said. Those precious secrets He reveals only to friends. *"I speak to you as my friends, and I have told you everything that my Father has told me."* (John 15:15). What is the business of the Father that Christ has revealed to us, as His friends?

The Father's business is the proclamation of the Son to the world, reconciliation of the creator to his creation through the Savior, Christ.

This is now your business, and my business.

As my own father has often preached: angels cannot come down from heaven and preach the Gospel. That is the mission of humans. Jesus is not coming back to this earth today to preach the Word. Instead, He has left *us* here — His *friends* — to do it. Telling our world about our Savior is the business of the kingdom, and that business has been placed into your hands and into my hands.

Telling our world about our Savior is the business of the kingdom.

Peter understood this instinctively in that moment when his brutal execution was prophesied by Jesus, and so he made no opposition to it. Later, in Acts 3, we find Peter and John extending the power of Christ to heal a crippled man by the gate called Beautiful. The miracle causes such a furor that the two disciples are arrested and called on to explain their actions. And here Peter gives the testimony that will define his ministry:

You are questioning us today about a kind deed in which a crippled man was healed. But there is something we must tell you and everyone else in Israel. This man is standing here completely well because of the power of Jesus Christ from Nazareth. You put Jesus to death on a cross, but God raised Him to life.

He is the stone that you builders thought was worthless, and now He is the most important stone of all. Only Jesus has the power to save! His name is the only one in all the world that can save anyone.

Acts 4:9-12

"His name is the only one in all the world that can save anyone." Peter has gone from a man who once had no idea of who Jesus was or what His purpose was, to a man who correctly identifies and preaches that there is no other name by which we must be saved.

Peter has been transformed from a servant of the Master into a friend. He finally understands the Father's business, and he is doing it.

I'm sure Peter had a fleeting thought that those who were judging him were about to condemn him to death. He probably thought, "I'm not that old, I thought I would have more time than this. But so be it, I know this business, I know my job."

Right now, Jesus calls you "friend." He has given you the Father's business to do, and He expects you to proclaim to your world that there is no other name under heaven by which we must be saved. He calls me "friend," and He expects me to be about the Father's business, too.

I know that the ministry of the *Book of Hope* is bearing fruit around the world, but not everyone supports the work.

We had a new neighbor on our block at home that I recently met for the first time. I told him about the ministry of giving scriptures to students around the world.

He seemed irritated by it and finally just came out and said, "Well, I think you're pretty arrogant. It's just like you Christians to think that these countries need you, that you have to go to these places and give out these books. These books won't feed them. They won't clothe them. You're wasting your time, and you're wasting your resources. You're wasting your money when you could be helping those people."

This is not an uncommon response to what we do. People say we are wasting resources to give God's Word to the children when we should be giving them food and clothing. My answer is this, and I believe it is the one Peter would have used ... Anyone can give the poor children food and clothing, but **only those who have been called to do the Father's business will give them God's Word.**

Jesus loved to feed hungry people. He did it a couple of times that we find recorded in the Bible. But when He gave His great commission to the disciples, He did not tell them, "Go ye into all the world and feed the hungry." He did not say, "Go ye into all the world and clothe the naked." Rather He said, *"Go ye into all the world, and preach the Gospel to every creature"* (Mark 16:15, KJV). That was His business, the business of the kingdom, and He made it our business when He called us His friends.

I believe Jesus wanted us to give humanitarian aid to the needy out of the compassion of our heart. As His death approached, He said, *"You will always have the poor with you, and whenever you want to you can give to them"* (Mark 14:7). The

Bible affirms again and again that those who help the poor will be blessed themselves, and even the commands of the Old Testament require that we give to those who are in need.

But Jesus did not die so that all the hungry could be fed. He did not die so that all the sick could receive medicine. He did not die so that all the poor could have warm clothes. He laid down His life upon Calvary as a sacrifice for our sins, so that all our souls could be saved. He said, *"What will you gain, if you own the whole world but destroy yourself? What would you give to get your soul back?"* (Matthew 16:26).

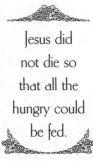

Jesus did not die so that all the hungry could be fed.

Saving souls is the Father's business. Jesus gave us that commission when He called us His friends. When we bear fruit for the kingdom, that fruit is measured in terms of souls.

If we feed every starving child in Africa, but fail to bring them into God's kingdom, we have done them no favors — they will still spend eternity in hell. If we build a home for every homeless person in America but fail to lead them to Jesus, we have not changed their future significantly — eternal separation from God is still their fate. If we get the best medicine to the worst-off victims of disease and disaster but fail to introduce them to the One who can heal their souls, they will still be doomed forever.

Our business is the business of fruit for the kingdom of God, the Father's business. While we should do what we can to ease the physical needs of our brothers and sisters in Christ, and those who are lost, too, our main concern is that we bear fruit that lasts for the kingdom of heaven. Food doesn't last.

Clothes don't last. Medicine doesn't last. **Souls last.**

Our main concern is that we bear fruit that lasts for the kingdom of heaven.

Now you have the right vision of Jesus. You know He is not the all-tolerant and Santa Claus Savior of everyone who tries to be good, but is, in fact, the only way to salvation. There is no other name. And now you know that He has a vision of you: He calls you His friend and commissions you to do the Father's business.

Let me tell you one other detail you may not know about Him. He is keeping score.

Now you are thoroughly confused, right? I have spent most of these pages convincing you that only the spiritual is important in light of eternity, and that we must not confuse spiritual principles for bearing fruit in the kingdom with physical principles for getting personal wealth. Am I doing a 180 on you and turning into a bean counter? What do I mean by the idea that God is keeping score?

Read on, and you'll see. Just because the eternal things are also the spiritual things — just because the important things are usually the unseen things — doesn't mean that they don't have a quantifiable value to God.

Chapter 9

SCORE KEEPER

I was as uncomfortable as I could be. Somehow I had been invited to lunch with a pastor of a huge, wealthy church and two other missionaries. It was obvious that the three of us missionaries were to present our cases to the pastor and hope that his congregation could support us.

I love the *Book of Hope* ministry, but I am not that competitive to enjoy trying to wring another dollar out of a compassionate church at the expense of some other worthy ministry. I decided to let this go, and just try to enjoy my lunch. I didn't say much as the other two missionaries described their works.

Finally, one of them turned to me and said, "Well, Rob, your ministry had a pretty big event not long ago, right?"

We had — and that was one thing I was happy to talk about! Just a few weeks before, we had given our children's scripture book to the 100 millionth child to receive it! In less than 15 years of the *Book of Hope*, we had reached more than 100 million students with God's Word. I described the circumstances of the 100 millionth child. He was an 11-year-old boy named Misha, from the little town of Chita, way in the east of Russia.

When he brought the *Book of Hope* home from school, his great-grandmother broke down and cried. She said that her father had been in the Red Guard, and after the Bolshevik Revolution, he never let the Bible be read again in their house. No one was ever allowed to pray. She said that she had often wished in her life that she knew how to pray. She had grown up wishing that she could believe there was a God who cared for her.

Misha was the first child in three generations in that home to have his own copy of the scriptures. There was a lot more to the story — Misha and his grandmother and great-grandmother made a commitment to Jesus. Misha's extended family was caught up in the excitement that he, of all the boys in the world, was the 100 millionth student to receive the *Book of Hope*.

When our partner church in that area of Russia went to the local government to apply for a permit to open a new church for the boys and girls and families who had come to Christ after the *Book of Hope* arrived, they found out that Misha's uncle was the one who had to approve their permit! Of course, they had no troubles at all ...

> He finally cut me off by saying, "That is just like you Americans! Always *quantifying*."

As I poured out my heart about the 100 millionth child, one of the other missionaries became rather put out with me. He was from another country, and he finally cut me off by saying, "That is just like you Americans! Always *quantifying* everything, as if *numbers* are that important."

He seemed to think numbers were sordid, and that keeping track of numbers was wrong. I didn't take up the point with him. I went back to my uncomfortable silence. But I believe in my heart that it's not just

Americans who are quantifying everything. I believe God quantifies everything, too.

Jesus stood by the temple, watching what everyone dropped into the collection box. Does that sound like someone who is not keeping score?

I don't know how God keeps records in Heaven. I don't think there's any way the most incredible programmers, mathematicians, or statisticians could ever create a database that would be able to keep track of fruit and spiritual lineage — how much God entrusted to us and what we did with it.

But I do know that there will be rewards meted out in heaven based upon what we did with the resources entrusted to us, and what kind of fruit was raised from the seeds we planted.

> *Whatever we build on that foundation will be tested by fire on the day of judgment. Then everyone will find out if we have used gold, silver, and precious stones, or wood, hay, and straw.*
>
> *We will be rewarded if our building is left standing. But if it is destroyed by the fire, we will lose everything. Yet we ourselves will be saved, like someone escaping from flames.*
>
> 1 Corinthians 3:12-15

How else can we see and rejoice in the spiritual lineage God has raised up through us on this earth, unless someone is keeping track of it?

In the mind of God, there is a super database that tracks everything. We cannot quantify in this life what we have done with our talents and abilities, and we will not know before that day of judgment what our reward will be. But the Scripture makes clear that it is based on results, on the fruit for the kingdom that can be attributed to us.

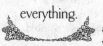

In the mind of God, there is a super database that tracks everything.

Our little Scripture book, the *Book of Hope*, costs only about 33¢ per student to provide to the children and youth in Latin America and the Caribbean, Russia and Eastern Europe, and some nations of Africa and Asia. Now there's a bonanza for somebody — every dollar plants the seeds of the Gospel message in three children.

I think about a little girl in Nicaragua — at 11 years old, she was raising her three younger brothers alone, none of them out of third grade yet. Their dad left the family and went to America. Their mom abandoned them and went to Costa Rica.

Every morning, this little girl was up at four, making tortillas that she sold during the day. She had to quit school, of course, and she was tired, afraid and hungry all the time. Finally, it was too much for her. She decided there was no way out except suicide.

There is a lot of despair in the poorest parts of Nicaragua, and she had heard about a new, easy way that people had been killing themselves. There was a chemical used to flash-freeze produce, but people had discovered if you ate it, it would freeze your lungs. It was a quick, almost painless way to die. She thought she could do it.

She knew she would go to hell because of it. She didn't have a relationship with Jesus, but from the little religious background her parents had given her, she knew suicide was a sin. What worried her was what would happen to her brothers. She was afraid that if they felt abandoned by her, as she felt abandoned by their parents, they might commit suicide, too — and end up in hell.

After struggling with this terrible thought, in great emotional agony and turmoil, she decided that she would kill her own brothers. She was going to hell anyway, she reasoned, if she killed herself. But at least her brothers would go to heaven.

The day that she made her painful decision, her little brothers came home from school with the *Book of Hope*. "Sister, sister!" they cried. "We got this book at school today! Will you read it to us?"

"Sister, sister!" they cried. "We got this book at school today! Will you read it to us?"

She sat down with them to read the book. It told the life story of Jesus, and explained to her how much Jesus loved her, and how she could have hope for the future. Right there, this little girl and her three brothers all prayed to accept Christ as Savior. Then they went to the church that had sent volunteers with the book to their school.

Now, I wonder, in God's great database, who gets credit for that beautiful fruit in the kingdom?

In Mark 4:26-29, Jesus said:

"God's kingdom is like what happens when a farmer scatters

seed in a field. The farmer sleeps at night and is up and around during the day. Yet the seeds keep sprouting and growing, and he doesn't understand how. It is the ground that makes the seed sprout and grow into plants that produce grain. Then when the harvest season comes and the grain is ripe, the farmer cuts it with a sickle."

Somebody gave a dollar to provide the *Book of Hope* for three children somewhere in the world, and they didn't know when they sent their check where those kids would be or what their needs would be. But they sowed their seed, and the word of God sprang up and took hold in those children.

God knows where each seed that you have sown has fallen, and He watches the way that it grows. ***Your spiritual lineage might extend around the world for all you know.***

In some ways, I dread the idea of judgment day and the final accounting of the fruit that I brought into the kingdom ... I have been so blessed, and I know that so much will be required of me. And yet in another way, I look forward to seeing how my spiritual lineage has expanded in ways and places that I never dreamed possible through the resources I contributed, the sermons I've preached, and other ways I can't even imagine.

Forget about asking Jesus for wealth and cars and real estate. How can anything like that compare to the spiritual lineage He is willing to give you? When you ask in accordance with the Jabez prayer, ask for something really BIG — something eternal!

~~~✿~~~ *Chapter 10* ✿~~~~~

ASK BIG

When my dad got *The Prayer of Jabez* book as a gift months ago, he and I were both amazed by how it confirmed a feeling that had been growing in our hearts over the past few years. It is the feeling that we have not accomplished as much as we could have for the kingdom simply because we haven't asked for it — the feeling that **the impossible is imminently possible for God, if we just ask for His help.**

When our hearts and motives are pure before the Lord, when we are living in His word and obeying His commands, then it is our Father's good pleasure to give us the kingdom! Already in our *Book of Hope* ministry, we had seen that there are no obstacles to how God can open doors and break down barriers.

I won't give you all the wonderful examples I could give you here, because that would fill up several more books. But I'll mention one of the most dramatic.

Our missionaries had made an appointment for me to meet with the ministry of education for the Philippines, and I was to ask for permission to bring the *Book of Hope* to every child and youth, right in their schools.

Before I left on the trip, I told my dad, "I don't think he'll say yes, but if he does, I don't think I should make any commitments. Our budget is stretched as tight as it can be this year, and we just can't take on anything else."

My dad sort of sat back and said, "Who are you to say no to Jesus? This isn't your ministry. It's not my ministry. It's not our denomination's ministry. This is God's work. Why not ask God for the Philippines?"

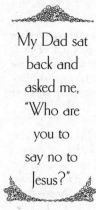

My Dad sat back and asked me, "Who are you to say no to Jesus?"

So I flew off to the Philippines with that rebuke in my heart, but with no real hope that we would get permission. I thought the finances would not even be an issue.

The vice-minister of education told me he knew the Bible and prayer had been outlawed in the schools of America, and he would not allow the *Book of Hope* into the schools of the Philippines, either. I said, "It's true that we made that decision in the schools of America, and now we have to live with the consequences."

I described to him how in the years since God and the Bible had been removed from school, the U.S. had begun to suffer from violence in the schools, teen pregnancies, drugs, diminishing test scores, and an overall decline in morals, values and academics.

He said, "The same thing is happening here," and he began to share statistics about teen violence and immorality in the Philippines.

You could almost feel the exact moment the Holy Spirit

invaded that room and convicted that man that the children and youth of his nation needed God's word. He called his secretary in and dictated a letter giving us access to take the *Book of Hope* into every school in the Philippines.

We would need to reach 7.2 million students.

"Can you do that?" he asked.

God had already knocked down one barrier, but everything in my humanness screamed, "No way!" But I heard, "Yes, we can" come out of my mouth, knowing we could do nothing, but God can do anything.

As soon as I could, I called my dad and told him: good news, bad news. They said yes, but now we need $2.2 million to provide the *Book of Hope* for every student in the Philippines.

My dad started laughing on the other end of the phone line, and he told me he was holding a check for $2 million in his hands. While I had been gone, he had met with a businessman that neither of us had ever heard of before, and that man had given him a commitment for more than we needed to reach all of the Philippines.

We have not because we ask not! When you ask in line with God's will, bearing fruit for the kingdom and obeying His commands, He does answer.

All right, one more example from our work. In the nation of Kosovo, the minister of education outright refused our requests to bring the *Book of Hope* into the schools after order had finally been restored there. He said, "This is a Muslim nation, and we will not have the Christian scriptures in the schools."

Our missionary coordinator tried every tack he knew, and finally just asked straight out: "What possible way could this ever happen?"

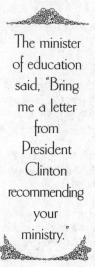

The minister of education said, "Bring me a letter from President Clinton recommending your ministry."

The minister of education, exasperated with the man's persistence, said, "Bring me a letter from President Clinton recommending your ministry." Say what you will about Bill Clinton, he sent troops to Kosovo to protect the ethnic Albanian Kosovars from the Serbians, and the Kosovar people love him.

When the missionary called me, pretty much defeated, he related that business about Clinton more or less as a joke. We knew there was no way Bill Clinton would recommend that the Bible be admitted to the classrooms of Kosovo. But a young fellow in our ministry headquarters wrote to the president and described what we wanted to do in Kosovo:

It was called Kosovo Peace Tour 2000, and it was an event that would combine youth concerts and entertainment with distribution of a book that would help the next generation in Kosovo find peace in the aftermath of war.

What do you know? President Clinton wrote back with a wonderful note that commended us for the good will effort we were making toward Kosovo!

That letter was presented to the minister of education, and he opened the doors for the *Book of Hope* in the schools of

Kosovo. **God's power and blessing is available to us if we just ask for it. He will even use the unlikeliest sources to bring that blessing about.**

When we are bearing fruit for the kingdom, resources are not the problem. God has riches beyond our wildest imagination. Man-made barriers are not the problem, because God has the ability to knock down any wall. Spiritual warfare is not the problem, because when we pray and intercede, God fights for us.

The only problem that I can see is that we fail to obey and we fail to ask. As Bruce Wilkinson points out in *The Prayer of Jabez*, "Even though there is no limit to God's goodness, if you didn't ask Him for a blessing yesterday, you didn't get all that you were supposed to have. There's the catch — if you don't ask for His blessing, you forfeit those that come to you only when you ask."

James 4:2-3 (NIV) says, *"You do not have, because you do not ask God. When you ask, you do not receive, because you ask with wrong motives, that you may spend what you get on your pleasures."*

When Jesus promised the answers to our prayers, He prefaced that with the qualification that we had to ask for them ... *"If you remain in me and my words remain in you, **ask** whatever you wish, and it will be given you"* (John 15:7, NIV). *"You did not choose me. I chose you and sent you out to produce fruit, the kind of fruit that will last. Then my Father will give you whatever you **ask** for in my name"* (John 15:16).

So, how do you activate the spiritual manifestations of the Jabez blessings in your life? **With a pure heart and motive**

before God, simply ASK!

Okay, and would it be so wrong to slip in a request for a newer car, a bigger house, or a million dollars, too? Absolutely not. If the new car is going to enable you to take the neighbor kids to church, go for it. If the bigger house is going to allow you to provide a home for your aging parents, then pray away. If you're going to sow a million dollars into ministries that are doing the Father's business, then I hope you get that million.

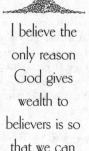

I believe the only reason God gives wealth to believers is so that we can bless others.

I believe the only reason God gives wealth to believers is so that we can bless others. I think of a fellow who used to give $50 a month to the *Book of Hope* ministry, and then one day he called and wanted to give a really, very generous donation. I looked over his records here at the office and saw that recently he had given far above his $50 monthly gift, and I asked what was going on.

He said when he first started giving that $50, he didn't really have it. He was broke. His wife was dying from cancer.

So in these difficult financial circumstances, he began to give money that he couldn't really afford to give, sometimes going without in order to keep up his commitment. And after a while, things looked better for him. Business picked up. He started giving even more. His wife recovered from cancer. Today, his business dealings have been blessed beyond belief. And he is still giving great gifts to ministries that are bearing fruit for the kingdom.

But no particular prayer activated those blessings in his life. He showed God that he could faithfully sacrifice in order to sow seeds for the kingdom ... and then God responded by entrusting more to him. He kept giving, and in return, God kept giving.

I don't expect this man was more worthy of blessing than old Adoniram Judson, and Judson's wife and children who died on the mission field. Some people get healed. Some people get rich. God uses each of us in different ways, but He can only use us when we decide to pray for and accept what God wants for us.

If you firmly believe that God wants to answer your Jabez prayer by giving you great material wealth, keep in mind that it would probably be a good idea, in addition to praying, to show God that you'll be faithful to use your wealth as He directs. Start giving today.

Ask big, and give big!

I am asking God for South Africa today, and I encourage you to join me in this prayer. Nothing has touched my heart quite the way the desperation of this nation has. The problems are myriad: recovering from the apartheid system and race reconciliation, tribal strife and breakdown of the tribal system, crime and violence out of control. But to me the scariest affliction for South Africa and many other nations of Africa is the AIDS epidemic.

At this moment, the sheer physical dimensions of the problem are daunting:

- There are 4.2 million infected with AIDS in South Africa alone, and that the HIV-infection rate includes nearly 20% of the entire population.

- Further, AIDS is decimating women in Africa — in 10 years in South Africa, the gender balance will be 60% men and 40% women with negative population growth.

- In some of the worst hit areas, HALF of all today's teenage girls will die of AIDS.

- Botswana had the highest AIDS rate in the world, and it *rose* by 38% in the year 2000 — 26% of pregnant girls age 15-19 in Botswana are already HIV positive.

- In nations like Botswana, Swaziland, Namibia and Zimbabwe, the AIDS virus will cut life expectancy to under 35 years of age by 2010.

- In one instance, a missionary in Zambia conducted AIDS testing for 200 schoolgirls, and all but 4 tested HIV positive!

- Almost 2/3 of the 34 million people with AIDS world wide live in sub-Saharan Africa.

- At the end of 1999, there were 12.1 million AIDS orphans in sub-Saharan Africa, and 430,000 children under age 15 died from AIDS in 1999 alone.

The young people of Africa have been forced to think about life and death. They are walking death sentences themselves. We don't have to convince these children that they need to prepare for death. We don't need to convince them that they need spiritual answers. They know it. And they are reaching out for help.

The *Book of Hope* is already being given to the students of many nations of Africa, and in South Africa, we are seeing dramatic life transformations already. My parents recently returned from a missions trip in Africa, and the report of the ministry was stunning.

During one three-day period in Cape Town, we gave the *Book of Hope* to 70,000 students in 65 schools, and 2,000 young people made a commitment to Christ, right at their school. Between 70% and 80% of those students were Muslims!

The very first township in South Africa to receive the *Book of Hope* was Delft, and the church that was working with us there has already experienced 40% growth. The children's ministry has grown from 60 kids to 200 — the youth from 24 to 120!

These kids are so ready for the word of God, and we know that it changes lives, hearts and behaviors.

> These kids are so ready for the word of God.

I wish I could solve all of their physical needs. I wish I could provide medicine to everyone to ease their suffering and prolong their lives. I wish I were a scientist that could come up with an immediate vaccination to save them from their physical plight. I can't — they are dying by the thousands every day. But I do know my business. It is the Father's business, it is an eternal business.

Lord, we ask you for the souls of the children of South Africa as an inheritance. We ask you that as we respond in obedience not one child will face eternity without a message of eternal hope. We are asking for all of South Africa.

As you feel God leading you to pray for the children and youth of South Africa, please do it! **You can add them to your spiritual lineage as they come into the kingdom of God!**

~~&~~ *Chapter 11* ~~&~~

FINALLY

*Finally, brothers, we instructed you how to live in order to please God, as in fact you are living. Now we ask you and urge you in the Lord Jesus to **do this more and more**.*

1 Thessalonians 4:1, NIV

"Do this more and more," the apostle Paul instructed. In my personal journey through Jesus' confirmation of the prayer of Jabez, I have discovered that command is very important: do this more and more. Success builds success.

It's difficult, at first, to launch out in faith. As Bruce Wilkinson puts it in *The Prayer of Jabez*, "It's a frightening and utterly exhilarating truth, isn't it? As God's chosen, blessed sons and daughters, we are expected to attempt something large enough that failure is guaranteed ... unless God steps in."

God's real glory is revealed when He accomplishes for us something that could *never* otherwise have been accomplished! If we attempt only what we can certainly achieve in our own human power, then we have no need of God's touch. But when we launch out by faith to do something crazy and

> When we launch out by faith to do something crazy and impossible, God alone is glorified in our success.

impossible, God alone is glorified in our success.

Do this more and more.

Peter worked far above his human potential, wouldn't you agree? When he abandoned himself to Jesus' plan for him, he also abandoned his own inability. A humble fisherman of little education saw no reason that Jesus couldn't make him one of the founding fathers of a church that would revolutionize the world and lead millions into eternity in heaven.

Abandon yourself to Jesus, and abandon your limitations, too. Those are *your* limitations, not God's.

And remember, Jesus has called you "friend" because He has revealed the Father's business to you and commissioned you to do it. You have the same kind of flaws and the same kind of potential that Peter had, and you can be used as greatly when you set your heart on doing the Father's business, the business of building the kingdom.

Give up your ideas of what should happen in this physical world.

God wants to bless you indeed. Jesus wants to answer your every prayer. And it is all easily possible, when you remain committed to bearing fruit, much fruit, fruit that will last.

Look back to our example of the apostle Peter. It shows you exactly how to activate the blessings God has for you.

• Give up your ideas of what *should* happen in this physical world according to your will. Remember, Peter gave up his hopes for a physical kingdom when he finally under stood the true nature of Jesus.

We have to give up on the idea that the promises of Jesus apply to material possessions and fleeting gain in this physical world and call on Him to unleash their power to bring about fruit that will last in the spiritual world.

- Totally abandon yourself to Jesus, and allow Him to use you in whatever way He wants to. When Peter recognized Jesus on the shore of the Sea of Tiberius, he flung himself into the ocean without a thought for who might see him or what they might think of him. His only thought was on being with the Master.

The physical world around him did not matter anymore. He had grasped the truth that would be written in Second Corinthians 4:17-18 (NIV), *"For our light and momentary troubles are achieving for us an eternal glory that far out-weighs them all. So we fix our eyes not on what is seen, but on what is unseen. For what is seen is temporary, but **what is unseen is eternal**."*

- Whatever the circumstances, accept them with faith that as long as you are yielded to God, He has promised that you will bear fruit for the kingdom, much fruit, fruit that will last!

Jesus prophesied Peter's death as a martyr, and Peter accepted it with no questions asked. Adoniram Judson knew he was dying without ever having achieved his vision of evangelizing Burma, yet he said that he moved on to heaven with bright prospects and warm feelings.

If you had high hopes that a nice formula like the prayer of Jabez was going to get you on God's good side and produce for you a better home, a bigger bank account and a nicer car, I hope this new perspective on the subject doesn't discourage you. And who knows — maybe those things are in your future anyway.

But I hope that whether they are or not, you now recognize that as much as you think you would enjoy the material blessings of wealth, they are ephemeral and fleeting. A far better investment of your time and resources would be in raising a spiritual lineage that you will carry with you from this life into the next.

When you set your sites on that prize, *Jesus has promised to help you with fruit, much fruit, fruit that will last.* When the bright morning of eternity dawns for you, I hope that it arrives with a legacy of souls that you brought with you into the kingdom, the testament to your commitment to do the Father's business.

That is the only really important thing.

Just a few years ago, our ministry celebrated the milestone of placing the *Book of Hope* into the hands of the 50 millionth child to receive it. She was a beautiful little girl from Peru named Tiffany, from a poor family in a poor *barrio* on the outskirts of Lima. There was a huge celebration in their neighborhood when the *Book of Hope* came to the local school, and Tiffany's whole family came into a relationship with Jesus Christ.

A couple years later, we heard that there had been great changes in the neighborhood since the distribution of the *Book of Hope* in Chorrillos, so we sent a video team back to follow up on Tiffany. What they discovered brought tears to our eyes. Yes, Tiffany was still serving God — she was on the youth outreach team and helping teach in children's church. But there was more.

At her school, a public school, the senior class from the year we distributed the *Book of Hope* had chosen my dad's name as their "saint's name" for the graduating class, and chosen me as their patron. About half the teachers and more than half the students had accepted Christ as Savior and were living for Jesus and attending church. There was a permanent plaque posted in their school, honoring the new hope that the *Book of Hope* had brought to their neighborhood.

The local pastors found that attendance in their churches had doubled, even tripled, and the youth groups and children's ministries had grown by leaps and bounds.

God's word had done all this. The many new Christians of Chorrillos are part of my spiritual lineage, and the lineage of my dad, and the supporters of the *Book of Hope* ministry, the volunteer teams that helped with the distribution, as well as our partner pastors, the team in our offices in the U.S. and in Latin America, and probably a host of people who I don't even know, who played a part in that miraculous story.

I don't know what anyone was praying when they sent their contribution to place the *Book of Hope* into the hands of the children of Peru, but if they were praying that they would bear fruit, much fruit, fruit that would last for the kingdom of God, then their prayers were answered.

Jabez got a promise from God, and he held onto it. Jesus gave a promise to you ...

*"You did not choose me. I chose you and sent you out to produce fruit, the kind of fruit that will last. **Then** my Father will give you whatever you ask for in my name"* (John 15:16).

Then the Father will give you whatever you ask. Hold onto that promise, bear fruit for the kingdom, and *then* you will receive whatever you ask in Jesus' name — and raise a rich spiritual lineage that will follow you from this physical world into the eternal world to come.

~~✦~~ Author's Note ~~✦~~

While this book was being readied for publication, Bruce Wilkinson's latest, *Secrets of the Vine* became available, with its insightful teachings on the promises of Jesus in John 15. If you enjoyed *THEN*, you will also want to get *Secrets of the Vine* by Bruce Wilkinson, and of course, *The Prayer of Jabez*, also by Bruce Wilkinson.

How many ways do you hope?

- We **hope** and pray.
- We wait and **hope**.
- We know that faith is the substance of things **hoped** for, and so sometimes...
- We **hope** against **hope**.

But at the end of the day, what gives *you* **hope**?

Now there's a FREE daily devotional that will give you a daily dose of inspiration and **HOPE**.

It's called *There's Hope for Today*, and it's our free gift to you.

Don't wait another minute for **hope**. Call or visit the website to get your FREE daily devotional, *There's Hope for Today!*

FREE devotional!
Daily inspiration from talented author Rev. David B. Crabtree and great stories of God's life-saving power. Call or write for it today!

Call toll free • 8:30-4:30 Eastern time
1-800-GIV-BIBL (448-2425)
Book of Hope International
3111 SW 10th Street
Pompano, Florida 33069
www.bookofhope.net
www.spirituallineage.com

More powerful true stories of fruit that lasts for the kingdom of God!

www. book of Hope .net

You'll find:

- latest ministry news
- exciting testimonies
- special offers
- prayer requests
- links to other great missions ministries
- and much more!

Keep up with the Book of Hope around the world — and don't miss **Hoskins Worldwide**

the international e-news update from Executive Director Rob Hoskins and ministry founder Bob Hoskins